ALPINE SKIING

GLOBAL CITIZENS: OLYMPIC SPORTS

Published in the United States of America by Cherry Lake Publishing
Ann Arbor, Michigan
www.cherrylakepublishing.com

Content Adviser: Liv Williams, Editor, www.iLivExtreme.com
Reading Adviser: Marla Conn MS, Ed., Literacy specialist, Read-Ability, Inc.

Photo Credits: ©Martynova Anna / Shutterstock.com, cover; ©Rrrainbow / Shutterstock.com, 5; ©Digitalt Museum, Norway/ Wikimedia Commons / Public Domain, 6; ©Polish NAC Archive / Wkikimedia Commons / Public Domain, 7; ©reinkadesign / Shutterstock.com, 8; ©FooTToo / Shutterstock.com, 10; ©Krzysztof Golik / Wikimedia Commons, 13; ©Olha Insight / Shutterstock.com, 14; ©Mitch Gunn / Shutterstock.com, 15; ©Iurii Osadchi / Shutterstock.com, 16; ©Kvanta / Shutterstock.com, 19; ©Jeff Smith - Perspectives / Shutterstock.com, 20; ©Lauren Proctor / Shutterstock.com, 21; ©OSZ Studio / Shutterstock.com, 22; ©Painted by Seo Munbo [late 15th century] / Wikimedia Commons / Korea Copyright Commission / Public Domain, 23; ©Photo from Italian magazine Avanguardia [1956] / Wikimedia Commons / Public Domain, 24; ©eWilding / Shutterstock.com, 27; ©PHOTOMDP / Shutterstock.com, 28

Library of Congress Cataloging-in-Publication Data

Names: Labrecque, Ellen.
Title: Alpine skiing / by Ellen Labrecque.
Description: Ann Arbor, Michigan : Cherry Lake Publishing, 2018. | Series: Global citizens: Olympic sports |
    Includes bibliographical references and index.
Identifiers: LCCN 2017029638 | ISBN 9781534107502 (hardcover) | ISBN 9781534109483 (pdf) |
    ISBN 9781534108493 (pbk.) | ISBN 9781534120471 (hosted ebook)
Subjects: LCSH: Downhill ski racing—Juvenile literature. | Winter Olympics—Juvenile literature.
Classification: LCC GV854.9.R3 L33 2018 | DDC 796.93/5—dc23
LC record available at https://lccn.loc.gov/2017029638

Cherry Lake Publishing would like to acknowledge the work of The Partnership for 21st Century Learning.
Please visit *www.p21.org* for more information.

Printed in the United States of America
Corporate Graphics

ABOUT THE AUTHOR

Ellen Labrecque has written over 100 books for children. She loves the Olympics and has attended both the Winter and Summer Games as a reporter for magazines and television. She lives in Yardley, Pennsylvania, with her husband, Jeff, and her two young "editors," Sam and Juliet. When she isn't writing, she is running, hiking, and reading.

TABLE OF CONTENTS

CHAPTER 1

History: Alpine Skiing

The first Winter Olympics was held in Chamonix, France, from January 25 to February 5, 1924. It included 258 athletes from 16 different countries competing in 16 events. Since then, the Winter Olympics has been held every 4 years in a number of countries. (The Games were skipped in 1940 and 1944 during World War II.) As the Games progressed, more competitors and events were added. Fast-forward to the 2014 Winter Games held in Sochi, Russia. There were 2,873 competitors from 88 different countries competing in 98 events. That's a lot more competitors and events!

From jaw-dropping aerial flips in snowboarding to lightning-speed action in hockey, the Winter Games display some of the most unbelievable sports and athletes. Alpine skiing, one of

The first Winter Olympics were known as "Winter Sports Week."

the fastest competitions in the Winter Olympics, draws some of the biggest crowds in all of the Games.

The Story of Skiing

Alpine skiing is an event where skiers race down steep mountains. It first became a sport in the Winter Olympics at the 1936 Games in Garmisch-Partenkirchen, Germany. The only alpine event held that year was the alpine "super combined." This means that one event consisted of two or more **disciplines**. In this case, the event combined one downhill race and two **slalom** races.

Alpine skiing made its Olympic debut at the fourth Winter Olympics in 1936.

Thirty-seven women from 13 nations competed in the alpine skiing events when they first debuted.

Before alpine skiing, there was Nordic skiing. It has been around since 3000 BCE! Unlike alpine skiers, Nordic skiers push themselves across flat ground. At first, it was just a way to travel through snow. It didn't become a sport until much later.

The term *alpine skiing* comes from the Alps, the giant mountain range in the middle of Europe. The first alpine skiers were people who enjoyed hiking in the Alps during the warmer months, but wanted to figure out a way to enjoy them in the winter months, too.

Skiing is popular in South Korea—most ski resorts stay open until 4:00 a.m.! Many expect it will gain even more popularity after the 2018 Games.

In 1850, Sondre Norheim of Telemark, Norway, invented the first toe and heel binding on skis. Previously, skis were just held on to people's boots by a flimsy strap. The toe and heel binding changed all this and really helped secure the skis on to people's boots. People started cruising down mountains without worrying about losing their skis.

The problem, though, was that once people skied to the bottom of the mountain, they had no easy way to get back to the top. Rope tows were used at first. They started popping up in the United States around 1934. This was the first motorized way

[21ST CENTURY SKILLS LIBRARY]

Events

At the 2018 Winter Olympics in PyeongChang, South Korea, alpine skiers will compete in several different events. Here's a rundown of what they are.

Men's and women's downhill	*Skiers compete against the clock to see who can finish the fastest.*
Men's and women's slalom	*A short race that includes sharp turns around flags.*
Men's and women's giant slalom	*A longer version of the slalom.*
Men's and women's Super-G:	*A longer, faster version of the giant slalom.*
Men's and women's alpine combined	*One downhill race followed by two slalom races—the combined best times wins this event.*
Team event	*Entire teams of both men and women compete against each other. It is a new event for 2018.*

for skiers to travel back up the mountain. The **chairlift** is what most skiers use today to get to the top of the mountain. It was invented shortly after the rope tow in 1936 at a ski resort in

According to a report, the 2022 Games in Beijing, China, will rely entirely on fake snow.

Sun Valley, Idaho. The lift easily elevated skiers up the mountain and helped make the sport more popular than ever.

Fake Snow

It's hard to ski without snow. So instead of waiting for snow to fall from the sky, Art Hunt, Dave Richey, and Wayne Pierce figured out how to invent their own snow. Fake snow, made by shooting water and pressurized air through a giant cannon, was first used at a ski resort in New York in 1952. Today, resorts and Olympic host cities all over the world rely on fake snow. At the 2014 Winter Games, Sochi created enough snow to cover 1,000 football fields!

Gathering and Evaluating Sources

Rope tows and chairlifts weren't invented until the mid-1930s, but people have been skiing since well before then. Using the Internet and your local library, gather information about the different ways skiers traveled back up the mountain before these mechanical systems were invented. Do you think this might be why alpine skiing wasn't introduced to the Winter Olympics until the 1936 Games? Why or why not? Use the information you find to support your answer.

CHAPTER 2

Geography: Skiing Around the World

At the 2014 Winter Olympics, 327 athletes from 74 nations participated in one of the alpine skiing events. Many of these skiers came from countries in Europe.

Where do the best alpine skiers in the world come from? Which countries have won the most Olympic alpine skiing medals?

Austria

Austria has dominated the Olympic alpine skiing scene. Its athletes have won 114 Olympic medals. No other country has won in the triple digits to date. Twice, Austria swept one event, winning the gold, silver, and bronze medals. They did it in the men's giant slalom in 1956 and the men's slalom in 2006.

Eva-Maria Brem of Austria represented her country at the 2010 Winter Olympics.

Mikaela Shiffrin (middle) won gold for the United States in the slalom event. Austria's Marlies Schild (left) and Kathrin Zettel (right) won silver and bronze.

When he was only 15, Maier was told he would never succeed in skiing.

Austria's Hermann Maier was one of the world's best alpine skiers. He won four Olympic medals in alpine skiing, including two gold in giant slalom and Super-G, at the 1998 Games in Nagano, Japan.

Switzerland

Switzerland has won 59 Olympic alpine skiing medals, including 20 gold. The Swiss have hosted the Winter Games twice: in 1928, before alpine skiing was included, and in 1948. At the 1948 Games, Switzerland won six alpine medals, including two gold.

Benjamin Cavet, a freestyle skier, competed at the 2014 Games for France.

France

France has won 45 medals in alpine skiing at the Winter Olympics, including 15 gold. The country has hosted the Winter Olympics three times: 1924 in Chamonix (prior to including alpine skiing), 1968 in Grenoble, and 1992 in Albertville.

Developing Claims and Using Evidence

The Alps mountain range stretches for 750 miles (1,207 kilometer) across eight countries. Look at a map of the mountain range and name the eight countries that are home to the Alps. Now, reread this chapter. Why do you think the top Olympic skiers come from Austria, Switzerland, and France? Using the Internet and your local library, gather more information to support your answer.

CHAPTER 3

Civics: Olympic Pride

Hosting the Olympic Games can be a big source of pride for the city and the people who live there. It gives the citizens a chance to show off where they live to the entire world. Also, the athletes and fans who come to the Games spend a lot of money there. One of the biggest ways the host country shows off is at the opening and closing ceremonies. More than 3 billion people watched the opening of the 2014 Winter Games!

The 2014 Sochi opening ceremony was a three-hour celebration of the Olympics and Russian history.

Skiing Popularity

More than 6 million people in the United States and over 2 million people in Canada ski every year. Not only do these people love to ski, but they love to watch it, too. Close to 27 million people in the United States watched downhill skiing at the 2010 Games in Vancouver, Canada. This was the second most popular sport to watch (just behind freestyle skiing).

A US Olympic freestyle skier trains in Park City, Utah, where the 2002 Games were hosted.

Whistler Blackcomb, the biggest ski resort in Canada,
hosted the alpine ski events at the 2010 Games.

Cutting Down Forests for the Slopes

The 2018 Winter Olympics is being held in PyeongChang, South Korea. The country and its citizens are excited about hosting the Games, but that excitement may have had an irreversible impact on an ancient forest.

The downhill and Super-G alpine skiing courses are being run on Mount Gariwang, home to a 500-year-old forest. More than 58,000 trees were torn down to clear the way for the slopes. The forest was home to many rare animals and plants like the

The South Korean government protected Mount Gariwang until 2013 in order to build the Olympic courses for the three-day alpine event.

lynx and different types of fir trees. The Olympic organizers promise to replant at least 1,000 trees after the Olympics. But many **environmentalists** feel like this isn't enough. They think the organizers should have built the slopes somewhere else.

Developing Claims

Go online and read more about the sacred forest on Mount Gariwang. Do you think PyeongChang should have tried to find a different skiing **venue** *for the 2018 Games? Why or why not?*

Mount Gariwang was under strict royal protection during the Chosun Dynasty in the late 14th century.

At the 1956 Games, Giuliana Minuzzo of Italy became the first woman to take the Olympic Oath, an event that happens during the opening ceremony.

Skiing for the Environment

Andrea Mead Lawrence was the first American alpine skier to win two gold medals at one Olympics. She won gold at the 1952 Games in Oslo, Norway, in the giant slalom and slalom. After she retired from competing in the Olympics, she became an environmentalist. She worked to preserve and take care of many mountains and rivers, including the Sierra Nevada in California. She saw the impact the Games were having on the environment. "Your life doesn't stop by winning medals," Lawrence said. "It's only the beginning. And if you have the true Olympic spirit, you have to put it back into the world in meaningful ways."

CHAPTER 4

Economics: Skiing Is Big Business

Hosting the Olympic Games costs a lot of money. PyeongChang has spent $1.5 billion on the ski resort for the 2018 Olympics! This doesn't include the cost of any of the other venues—even the stadium for the opening and closing ceremonies. The city hopes to earn back a lot of that money once the Games begin.

The Fans

Olympic **tourists** spend money by staying in hotels, buying souvenirs, and eating in the city's restaurants. People travel from near and far to see skiing's top athletes. The chance to see their favorite athletes is a huge draw for many fans. At the 2014 Games, more than 1 million tickets were sold and over 100,000 people visited the Sochi **Olympic Park**!

Olympic fans trickle in to the RusSki Gorki Jumping Center to watch the ski jumping events in 2014.

The Ambassadors

Olympic cities ask athletes to be **ambassadors** for their Games. The athletes promote the Olympics to fans around the world. One of the ambassadors of the 2018 Games is American alpine skier Lindsey Vonn. Many claim she is the most famous female skier in the world. Reaching speeds of 61 miles (98 km) per hour, Vonn is also the only American woman to win a downhill gold medal at the Olympics (Vancouver, Canada, 2010) to date. When she races in 2018, she'll definitely draw in the crowds.

Vonn is also sponsored by Red Bull, VISA, Audi, and HEAD as pictured here.

The Sponsors

Advertisers like Coca-Cola and McDonald's pay a lot of
money to sponsor the Olympics. Their signs and logos appear

Communicating Conclusions

*Before reading this book, did you know much about skiing and
the Winter Olympics? Now that you know more, do you think
alpine skiers should always try to go faster? Do you think this
would make the sport even more dangerous? Share what you
learned with friends at school or with your family at home.*

on television in commercials and on boards all over the venues. Clothing companies supply the athletes' uniforms and their outfits for the opening and closing ceremonies. The US Olympic skiing team also has its own sponsors, such as the outdoor clothing companies L.L. Bean and Spyder. Skiers have to wear the Olympic uniform, but they can use equipment and other gear made by other companies. Lindsey Vonn always skies with goggles made by Oakley. Oakley pays her money to do so. Fans of Vonn see her wearing these goggles, and it makes them want to buy a pair, too!

Taking Informed Action

Do you want to learn more about the Winter Olympics and skiing? There are many different organizations that you can explore. Check them out online. Here are three to help you start your search:

- US Alpine Ski Team: Learn more about the US Alpine Ski Team on its official website.
- Team USA—Alpine Skiing: Read about the athletes and qualifications for the US Olympic Team.
- Olympic—Alpine Skiing: Find out more about the history of alpine skiing at the Olympics.

Think About It

Today, Olympic skiers can ski over 60 mph (96.5 kph). In fact, Matthias Mayer of Austria had an average speed of 61.9 mph (99.6 kph) when he brought home the gold medal at the 2014 Games. Mayer was about 32 mph (51.5 kph) faster than Birger Ruud of Norway, the gold medalist at the first Olympic alpine event in 1936. Using the Internet and your local library, gather information about the differences between the recent Olympic alpine events and its skiers and when they first debuted. What factors may have led to skiers competing at faster speeds? Use the evidence you find to support your answer.

For More Information

Further Reading

Braun, Eric. *Lindsey Vonn.* Minneapolis: Lerner Publications, 2017.

Wallechinsky, David, and Jaime Loucky. *The Complete Book of the Winter Olympics.* Hertford, NC: Crossroad Press, 2014.

Waxman, Laura Hamilton. *Skiing.* Mankato, MN: Amicus Ink, 2017.

Websites

The International Olympic Committee
https://www.olympic.org/the-ioc
Discover how the IOC works to build a better world through sports.

International Ski Federation—Alpine Skiing World Cup
www.fis-ski.com/alpine-skiing
Learn more about skiing competitions all over the world.

GLOSSARY

ambassadors (am-BAS-uh-derz) representatives for something, like the Olympics

chairlift (CHAIR-lift) a series of chairs, suspended from a cable driven by motors, that take skiers up a slope

disciplines (DIS-uh-plinz) certain skills or fields of study

environmentalists (en-vye-ruhn-MEN-tuh-lists) people who work to protect air, water, animals, and plants from pollution and other harmful things

Olympic Park (uh-LIM-pik PAHRK) an area that typically contains the Olympic Stadium, venues for indoor sports, and housing for the Olympic athletes

slalom (SLAH-lohm) a speed race where skiers weave through a course of gates and tight turns

tourists (TOOR-ists) people who are traveling for pleasure

venue (VEN-yoo) the place of an action or event

INDEX

[21ST CENTURY SKILLS LIBRARY]